C000242416

Memories

of

Leigh

The publishers would like to thank the following

companies for their support in the production of

this book

Main Sponsor
Waterfields (Leigh) Limited

Browns of Leigh

Jim Stones Coaches

Waterlink Sutcliffe Group

First published in Great Britain by True North Books Limited
England HX3 6AE

Copyright © True North Books Limited, 2000
This edition reprinted 2007

All rights reserved. No part of this publication may be reproduced, stored in a retrieval system, or transmitted in any form, or by any means, electronic, mechanical, photocopy recording or otherwise without the prior permission in writing of the Copyright holders, nor be otherwise circulated in any form or binding or cover other than in which it is published and without a similar condition being imposed on the subsequent publisher.

ISBN 1 903204 27 5

Text, design and origination by **True North Books** *Limited*

Memories
of
Leigh

Contents

Introduction

'Holidays at home' was a wartime scheme designed to help keep the nation's workforce fit and healthy, as well as productive. Many areas continued the idea well into the 1950s.

A sk most Leigh folk how the place got its name and they probably won't know. No-one knows for certain, but the most likely explanation seems to be that it is just another way of spelling 'lea' meaning meadowland, or 'lee', meaning a sheltered place. Amalgamate the two and it seems a very fair description of Leigh. And the built up area we call Leigh is an amalgamation of the original focal points of farming settlements called Bedford, Pennington and Westleigh. In addition to their arable and pastoral farming of course the people living here spun thread and wove cloth in their homes.

With the development of mechanical techniques like the flying shuttle and the spinning jenny in the 18th Century, trade increased, spinning and weaving superseded farming and people in the three areas had more connections with each other. The 19th Century development of power-driven machinery and the move of the industry from the home into factories eventually resulted in the three areas and a strip of land in Atherton coming together and forming the Urban District of Leigh in 1894.

This was still governed as part of Lancashire County but five years later Leigh gained the right of incorporation. In future its eligible citizens would elect a Town Council which would levy its own rates to provide services and appoint professional officials to administer them.

Fifty years later civic pride was shown when special celebrations - and they were quite spectacular for 1949 - were staged to give expression to this pride. *Continued overleaf*

In the final week of September 1949, Leigh celebrated its half-century as an incorporated borough and the celebrations culminated in this spectacular parade on 1st October.

From previous page: One wonders if similar celebrations will take place in 2025 to celebrate Leigh's incorporation into the Metropolitan Borough of Wigan. It is a cliché to say the world is getting smaller and in the sphere of government nation states, not least the United Kingdom, are having to contemplate the prospect of amalgamating with other countries in some form of larger entity. People are always naturally anxious about losing their identity.

It is a refreshing thought however that alongside this move towards larger bodies politic, there is a move to preserve the corporate identity of small associations. The devolution of political power and the conservation of local heritage are encouraging trends that the identity of smaller units will not be obliterated by the larger.

May Leigh be part of that process. The town has much to be proud of in its past: Rugby League

players capped for England, an England Cross Country member, the deepest pit sunk in a colliery in the UK, Thomas Highs and his spinning jenny, Gerald Manly Hopkins, James Hilton and Alan Bullock in the world of letters, Tom Burke, Peter Maxwell Davies in music, Ken Platt in popular entertainment and many notable mechanical and engineering developments in industry.

It is hoped that this book will evoke proud and happy memories for people old enough to remember what life was like some time ago by looking at the photographs and that people who are too young to remember the scenes portrayed may gain some knowledge of what life was like in Leigh in the middle years of the 20th Century.

Leigh's motto of 'Aequo Pede Propera' or 'Hurry with equal feet' i.e. 'progress steadily' is well illustrated by the images of people in the past and no doubt will continue to be so in the future.

Street scenes

Market Street, Leigh about half a century ago seems an oasis of calm and quiet compared with the hustle and bustle one encounters today. Where is all the traffic? Where are the double yellow lines? Where are the Pelican Crossings? Where are all the street signs forbidding motorists to do this, that and the other? Pedestrians walking leisurely across and indeed, in the road, give a very different picture of what being in the centre of a town then was like compared with nowadays. And all the individual shops along both sides of the street: no great multiple chain stores then but family businesses with the family-owners probably living above their shop as most of the buildings in the photograph are more like normal dwelling homes than business premises. To go back just over a hundred years before this picture was taken however, Market Street was anything but calm and peaceful. It was here that the notorious 'Leighth Feight' occurred in August 1839. At the height of the Chartist agitation to try to obtain higher wages and better living conditions for working class people, a visit to Leigh by a well-known Chartist, the Reverend Stephens, had resulted in an excitable crowd gathering. Mills were attacked and the mob increased so that several special constables were enlisted by Squire Worthington and he read the Riot Act from the steps of the Obelisk. When a scuffle broke out at the front of the crowd, people at the back pushed forward whilst those at the front tried to escape. General pandemonium ensued until eventually the Constables got the upper hand. Many arrests and jail sentences followed.

Above: This view of King Street looking towards Market Street has several peripheral architectural features of interest as well as some interesting examples of vehicular transport. Architecturally, most buildings on both sides of the road are stolid, no-nonsense structures, almost seeming to declare 'we are here to stay'. Dominating the scene in the centre of the picture is the Rope and Anchor Hotel at the corner of Bradshawgate and Market Street, its peculiar onion-shaped dome giving it an almost East European aspect until below it one sees the stolid, undoubtedly British early 20th Century design. Similarly what was Burtons across from it, the white upper walls standing out above the earlier more domestic style buildings along the right side of King Street. Amongst the nearer row of shops was Yates and Greer's Pork Butchers, notable for having its own piggery to supply its 'raw material'. Despite appearing indestructible, this block was demolished to make way for the new Bus Station, but the George and Dragon Public House, in the centre of the picture is still there. The van on the left of the picture belongs to Greens, a bottling firm of Leigh, and its design, like the style of the three other motor vehicles, the sit-up and beg bicycle on the pavement and the trolley-bus approaching, surely date this picture to the 1940s or 1950s.

Both pictures: VE Day Street parties at Dakins Lea Estate, commemorate the end of the war in Europe in May, 1945. A beautiful Spring Day heralding the beginning of a new era that all had looked forward to for so long. The mothers in the picture would remember similar street parties in the previous decade: first when King George V and Queen Mary celebrated their Silver Jubilee in 1935, and then two years later when their son and daughter-in-law were crowned King George VI and Queen Elizabeth. (If they were school children then they would probably have two china mugs at home in commemoration of those events). Street parties were the traditional way of celebrating such important national events and what could be more significant than the end of six years of war. Of course, World War II was not over: the war in the Far East was still waging and would do so until the following August - but what was the Far East? Too far away to bother people in this country: the war against Japan was a matter for the Americans and Australians to take note of: Europe was now at peace so we could celebrate! The world was a much bigger far flung place in 1945 than it is today. No doubt many of the children seated round the tables would have participated as parents, in celebrating the present Queen's Silver Jubilee by organising a similar street party for their children in 1977, but also undoubtedly, the parties in 1977 would be much more abundantly provisioned. Rationing was still the norm in 1945 and many of the children pictured would not know what a banana was. A salutary thought for older people nowadays is that many of these children will now be pensioners and grandparents and the baby on the left of the picture will be fifty-five years old.

On the move

The transport depot at Callenders Cable Works shows the Company's cars and van on the left of the picture and the lorries with their peculiar 'tricycle style chassis' on the right. Judging by the number of ladies employed as drivers, this photograph may well date from the war years and certainly, judging by the design of the cars and the square-shaped trucks behind the lorries, it is not later than the 1950s. Callenders had the reputation of being a very self-contained firm, both in providing its own services and in the welfare for its employees and here are examples of both these aspects. On the left is a petrol pump (and in wartime this would be very strictly rationed) and on the right, behind the first lorry, is the canteen building. This part of the factory complex was also on the periphery of the site as it is very close to the residential housing running along the back of the photograph.

Above: A view of the platforms at Leigh Central Railway Station. The station looks particularly spick-and span and is bedecked with flags and bunting in celebration of some important national or local occasion. If local, it could be the commemoration of the fiftieth anniversary of Leigh's incorporation as a borough, but it is more likely to be the celebration of the present Queen's Coronation in 1953. The station does not look at all busy: three or four travellers with luggage who were presumably travelling from Leigh to a much bigger railway station like Manchester, and a station employee. The platform clock shows us the time was late morning. The fact that the station was not very busy makes us less surprised that it was one of the many closed by Dr Beeching in the 1960s. In the background of the picture is a typical Lancashire sight, a large mill chimney: but one also sees something that is not so typical, a water storage tower. This was built by Callenders Cable Works to provide them with an adequate supply of soft water. The local water pumped from the wells was hard and the pressure was unsuitable, so the Cable Works decided to supply their own.

Below: A group of dedicated Roman Catholics formally posing for a photograph on the platform of Leigh Railway Station prior to leaving for the journey to London to celebrate a Marian year. It was probably in the late 1940s, and yet again the dress of the people portrayed make it easy to date. Almost all the ladies are wearing hats and top coats and some of the gentlemen wear a trilby or a cloth cap. One shorter individual, presumably not old enough nor of the right gender to make the front rows, is determined not to be missed and raises an arm to make sure 'his' family and friends know that he was present. The engine on the left of the picture is already getting up steam to take the party on this excursion to London, a venture much more unusual and lengthy in those days than it would be today.

to let the founders down and the current generation remains committed to ensure that the legacy is not diluted as the business continues to grow.

The future of Waterfields now looks as rosy as its past. Just as we enjoy the privilege of recalling from our childhood the delicious smells of fresh dough and flour mingled with sugar, chocolate and the unmistakable scent of fresh bread so our children and our children's children will be able to share that same glorious experience; in their adult years they too will be able to look back and if they close their eyes recall the same happy memories themselves of being taken by their mothers to a real bakers and smell real bread rather than only having the sad memories of being dragged around a soulless supermarket with its cavernous aisles and bland products.

Surely generations yet to come will recall Waterfields Bakers with nostalgia and satisfaction; and some at least will spare a few moments thought for the firm's founders, Alice and Albert Waterfield, whose hard work made such pleasures possible.

experience and knowledge providing specialist training in craft, selling skills and related subjects for other bakery and confectionery businesses.

Despite the passing of so many decades the company is still very much a family business: John Waterfield is now Managing Director, Richard Waterfield is Chairman. Albert Waterfield retired in 1997 but still works a few days each week on specific directors' projects; Albert's wife Jean is now completely retired as is Hilda Hendry whilst Helen Fisher (nee Waterfield) controls all outside catering and Roger Hendry, Hilda' son, is buyer for the company.

Looking to the future Waterfields still believes that the company can grow further without compromising the goal of quality laid down by 'Mister' in the 1920s. The commitment to staff and the training they are given will continue to be crucial to that objective. The firm is strongly aware that customers come first and that quality is paramount. The grandchildren of the founders are only too well aware that losing sight of those two issues would be

Top left: *A training session taking place in Waterfield's own purpose-built Training Room.*
Above left: *Waterfield's Crompton Fold Site.*
Below: *Richard, Albert and John Waterfield.*

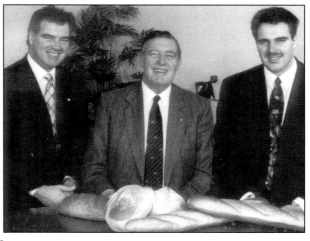

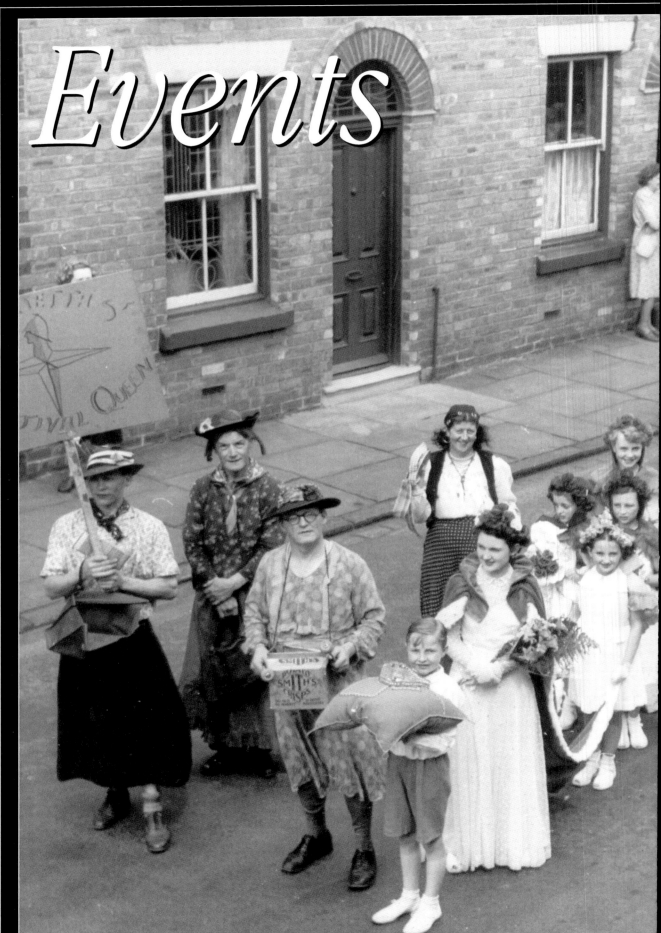

Events

Henrietta Street, Leigh, and part of a parade in 1951 to commemorate the Festival of Britain in that year. Britain was just about emerging from the years of austerity of the war years and the late 1940s and was still keen to celebrate the euphoria of that atmosphere. Of course, the Korean War was waging at this time and to those people who had been called up to do their National Service in 1950 for eighteen months, had their period of time in the forces extended to two years as a result, but for most people Korea was at the other side of the world and not really any of 'our' business. Let the Americans deal with that: we in this country had experienced six years of being 'in the frontline' during the . As regards Leigh in 1951, perhaps a parade was very much an accepted and expected event, it was only two years since the town had celebrated its golden jubilee as an incorporated borough and parading was the order of the day then. Pride of place in this procession is a Rose Queen and her retinue and the majority of the followers are children dressed up to represent 'fairy story' characters but towards the back of the parade is a wedding couple.

Grace Hewitt

Above: One of the floats from the 1949 Parade, commemorating fifty years of local government in Leigh. This was the display of the Leigh Swimming club which had been very successful if the numbers of trophies exhibited on the float is anything to go by. Being October 1st and judging by the apparel of the crowds lining the route of the parade in other photographs, it was obviously too chilly for the swimming club to appear in their usual costumes, or perhaps they were just modest. Their posters, however, urge people to make use of the Silk Street Baths, advising people 'for Health's Sake, Swim!'. The Baths in Silk Street date from 1881 but their site is now occupied by a car park and the nearest swimming baths for Leigh people are in Wigan.

Below: A beautiful picture of young girls dressed in white carrying bouquets of flowers. This must have been a church procession and probably one from an Anglican Church, maybe the Parish church, as the Roman Catholic Churches in Leigh did not walk in this way after the war - and the dress of the young girls and the ladies in the picture seems to date the scene in the late 1940s or 1950s. The buildings behind the procession are of some interest. The tower in the rear of the picture on the right is the old library and technical college building, which is still there on Railway Road but the verandah running along the premises in the centre of the picture has been removed. These premises are still occupied by various shops.

Another picture of the 1949 carnival: this time showing the motorised floats carrying displays reflecting life in Leigh. The leading vehicle is a truck belonging to Callenders, a famous and well respected firm of cable-manufacturers in Leigh. A typical traditional 'family concern' which had the reputation for good industrial relations: work people had the impression that they were well looked after with good canteen facilities and the provision of works' outings to various places. The Callender truck here is transporting the May and Rose Queens of Pennington Church. Similar 'floats' and carriages are featured in the parade behind it. This stretch of Leigh Road shows a typical mixed business of the time, Laylands in the double fronted shop and next to it a Newsagents/tobacconists shop displaying an advertisement for a well-known brand of cigarettes in 1949, Craven A. The number of chimney-stacks on the roofs of the houses is also very reminiscent of this era: all rooms in these houses would be heated, if at all, by solid fuel fires, and the amount of smoke and soot this discharged into the atmosphere must have been enormous. There are no television aerials to be seen however: few families possessed TV, the main media were still the radio, cinema, newsreels and newspaper.

In September, 1959, the Mayor of Leigh, Mr J Sumner, attended the Jubilee Celebrations of Leigh Harriers at Leigh Athletic Club. The Club House can be seen in the background of the picture behind the two parked cars. To the left of the Club House is Bonth's Spinning Mill, and together with the tall factory chimney set this scene as a typical one in Lancashire textile country. The occasion appears to be a fund-raising as well as a celebratory one with chocolates and biscuits on sale as well as other goods. Amongst the assembled crowd who are no doubt members or relatives of members of the club is Mr Matthew Thorpe, a well-known local athlete. He is standing at the front holding his trilby in his left hand.

Top: Lasses from Lancashire, according to the old ballad, were not only pretty but noted for wearing clogs and shawls. The old clog shop on King Street, Leigh, was the place where such footwear was manufactured. Of course, clogs were not just feminine footwear: men and children also had their own pair of clogs. Made from strong leather with a wooden platform on the base of which would be metal lines, clogs were made to be long-lasting and affordable to work people: they seldom needed repairing and when they did it would be to have new 'clog irons' to replace the worn or damaged lines. These clog irons were the reason for clog-dancing as they made the appropriate clatter which presumably was the origin of tap-dancing, and when the snow came in winter they provided children with endless fun 'skating' along the ice-slides constructed in the school playgrounds and also in collecting 'cloggy-boggies' on their bases which resembled walking on stilts. The building is interesting in that it has a thatched roof, very unusual in a factory town: no doubt today, it would have a Conservation Order to preserve it as a building of historical interest but it was demolished in the 1930s to make way for the Regal Cinema.

Above left (smaller picture): An unpretentious and apparently not very interesting public house but the building goes back to the late 18th Century and the Royal Oak Inn is remembered in the traditional folklore of Leigh. From 1779 the inn at the corner of King Street and Twist Lane, was owned by the Latham Family. In 1930 a local aristocrat named Henry Worsley persuaded the landlady to heat several copper coins which he then placed in the street. Some children eager to acquire this treasure got burnt in picking up the coins and there was a great disturbance. The landlady got an attorney who lived next door to

summon the Parish Constable who locked up Worsley in the pub's 'dungeon'. Worsley shouted loud offering rewards to the local people to pull down the building. Word got to Robert Worsley of Golborne who, together with other gentlemen, opened up the dungeon, releasing Henry. The attorney was summoned to court at Liverpool where he was fined and a complaint having been made to the Home Secretary, the government ordered the demolition of the dungeon which was 'not fit to keep a dog in'

Above: The 1949 parade celebrating the 1899 incorporation of Leigh. Fifty years on and only four years since the end of World War II, people throughout Britain felt the need to lighten the dark days of the years of austerity; rationing, clothing coupons and utility furniture were still the norm. any form of escapism was welcome; what better than to celebrate one's home town and civic pride. Some people love to dress up and here was a great opportunity to do so. If you could ride a horse, so much the better, you could be a cowboy (or cowgirl in this instance), if not then dress up as some character you admire and go on shanks' pony. In addition to the dress of the parade participants, it is also interesting today to notice the dress of the spectators. It was October 1st so not yet wintertime, but most people, both men and women, wear a top coat and headgear: nowadays the norm would be trousers for both sexes (probably jeans) and some form of anorak.

Below: Previous photographs of Chapel Street have shown it pictured from above: here we see part of it at ground level. A considerable amount of slum clearance had occurred on this side of Chapel Street, though the properties in the rear of the photograph are still there, one of which has an almost ecclesiastical appearance with its Gothic arched windows above the shop front. Work is now being started on the land from where the old properties were demolished: the workmen digging trenches for foundation stones, power supply lines or whatever. No mechanical diggers in use, but all hand labour. One man stands watching the gang doing the hard work: was he just a passer-by with nothing better to do or could he be the foreman ensuring that his charges got on with the job in hand? Across the road, two ladies out shopping ignore the activity on this side of the street, no doubt putting the affairs of the world to rights, or at least the affairs of Leigh. Ultimately, of course, they and all the other citizens of Leigh, would be aware of the fruits of the labours of the workmen as the Police Station and Law Courts were to emerge on this patch of land.

Above: Taken outside Plattfold Mill on a warm summer's day, this photograph epitomises work and leisure. The heavy dominant building of the factory is typical of the cotton mills built in Lancashire. This mill was also known as Bouth's Mill as Frederick Bouth had bought it in the 1890s and built a long row of houses along Plattfold Street to accommodate his workpeople. The mill prospered and specialised in the production of fine yarns. In the 1920s the firm was absorbed into the Fine Spinners Combine but it closed as a cotton mill in 1957. It was acquired by the firm named on the side of the mill in the picture in 1958 and its production was now of electrical equipment. Ward and Goldstone expanded to other places in the north and in Ireland and this led to specialisation, Leigh being responsible for the Appliance Assembly side of the industry. The photograph appears to be taken during a lunchtime with several of the employees enjoying a break in the warm summer atmosphere. Most of the employees seem to be female. In 1973 there was a threatened strike by female workers but strike action was averted with the promise of equal pay. Plattfold Mill closed in 1979, the business transferring to Hindley Green.

Right: Another internal picture of Callenders Cable Works in wartime: again only one man is seen and he appears to be of an age that would have excluded him from service in the armed forces. Here the job in hand is the testing of the cables: these were probably radio frequency cables being tested for their power-rating. The picture is dated 1944 but without the date, the young lady's hairstyle typifies the fashion adopted by ladies during the second world war.

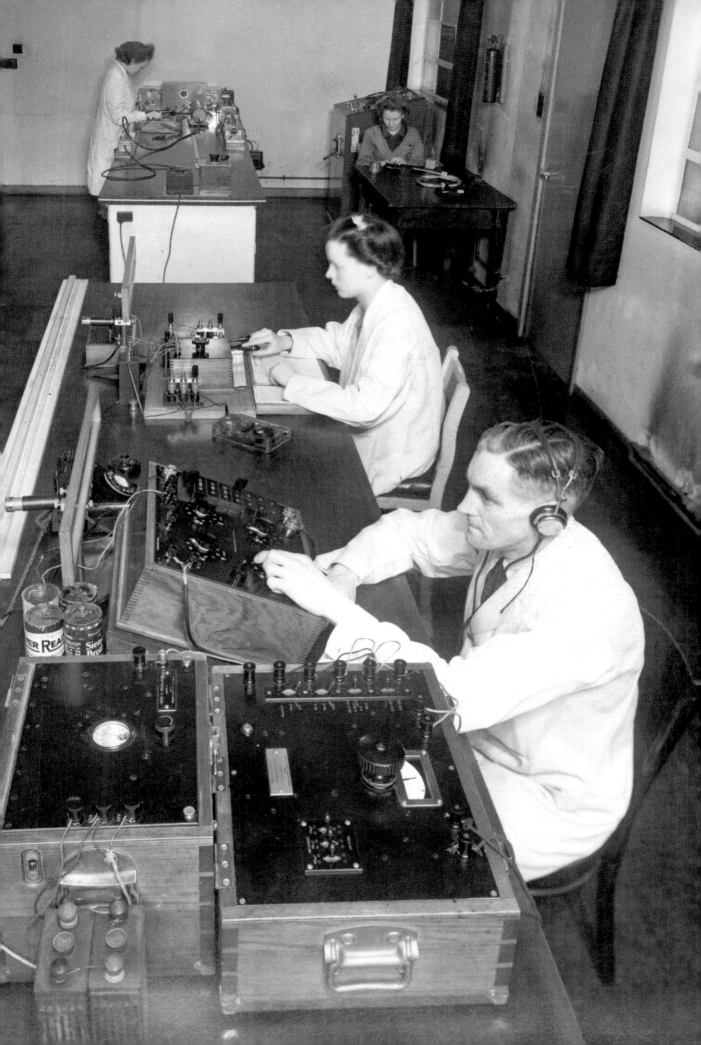